THE KNOPF POETRY SERIES

1   Robert Mazzocco, *Trader*

2   Cynthia Macdonald, *(W)holes*

3   Thomas Rabbitt, *The Booth Interstate*

4   Edward Hirsch, *For the Sleepwalkers*

5   Marie Ponsot, *Admit Impediment*

6   Brad Leithauser, *Hundreds of Fireflies*

7   Katha Pollitt, *Antarctic Traveller*

8   Nicholas Christopher, *On Tour with Rita*

9   Amy Clampitt, *The Kingfisher*

10   Alan Williamson, *Presence*

11   Stephen Sandy, *Riding to Greylock*

12   Pamela White Hadas, *Beside Herself*

13   Sharon Olds, *The Dead and the Living*

14   Peter Klappert, *The Idiot Princess of the Last Dynasty*

15   Mary Jo Salter, *Henry Purcell in Japan*

16   Norman Williams, *The Unlovely Child*

17   Marilyn Hacker, *Assumptions*

18   Amy Clampitt, *What the Light Was Like*

19   Cynthia Macdonald, *Alternate Means of Transport*

20   Brad Leithauser, *Cats of the Temple*

21   Edward Hirsch, *Wild Gratitude*

22   Brooks Haxton, *Dominion*

23   Mary Swander, *Driving the Body Back*

BOOKS BY MARY SWANDER

Needlepoint
Succession
Lost Lake

DRIVING THE BODY BACK

DRIVING THE BODY BACK

poems by

MARY SWANDER

Alfred A. Knopf   New York   1986

THIS IS A BORZOI BOOK
PUBLISHED BY ALFRED A. KNOPF, INC.

Some of the poems were originally published in *Crazy Horse, Open
Places, Poet & Critic,* and *The Reaper.*

Grateful acknowledgment is made to Almo/Irving Music Company for
permission to reprint an excerpt from the lyrics to "Boney Fingers."
Words and music by Hoyt Axton and Renee Armand. © 1973 Lady Jane
Music and Irving Music Inc. Used by permission.

*The author would also like to thank the Ingram Merrill Foundation, and
extend special thanks to Jane Staw for her encouragement and criticism
of these poems, and her support during the writing of this book.*

Library of Congress Cataloging-in-Publication Data

Swander, Mary. Driving the body back.

    I. Title.
PS3569.W253D75   1986   811'.54   85–45603
ISBN 0–394–55008–0
ISBN 0–394–74289–3 (pbk.)

Manufactured in the United States of America

FIRST EDITION

for Eileen Stone

Speak to the earth and it will teach thee.

—Job

CONTENTS

DRIVING THE BODY BACK

JIM

The road winds over hills,
gullies between fields,
as we drive my mother's body
back to the town
where we were born,
and you tell me how most
of the family rode home
to lie for months
on the cot in the front room.
Pulling himself up for the
first time in weeks, Uncle Jim
washed, shaved, dressed in
white collar and tie—
and began his tale
at one in the morning—
your turn to listen.
And until the sun rose,
hunks of meat swayed back
and forth in his butcher shop.
Hooves dropped into stewpots,
intestines, scraped clean,
were stuffed again,
then found gleaming from
the faces of frying pans,
the odor rising through the house.
Jim claimed he knew all
there was about animals—
how hide clings to muscles,
how a heifer harbors

a fetus, how the udder
sags, abdomen bulges,
and the first sign she gives
is so human: a swelling
the shape of a hand.
Under the skin, you can
almost trace the bones
of the fingers, the lines
stretching back toward the ribs.
When the priest stretched
his palms over Jim,
you could not find a match
for the candles, you could
not shoo the old man's parakeets
back into their cage
or remember the prayers
as you knelt by the cot,
and you could not stop laughing,
the birds darting about,
your missal falling open,
Latin blurring, cotton settling
on Jim's eyes, nose, lips.
It was December,
the ground sealed by snow,
the wake put off until the thaw.
You waited all winter,
the body rolled in blankets
and stored in the hayloft,
then in March,

Uncle George brought
the corpse into the house,
stood it up in the corner
and poured whiskey down
its throat, then hands
shuffled through hands
and the squeeze-box wheezed
till early morning.
When the mourners finally
trickled out, once again
the storm door flew open,
clouds gathered, the wind
sang and you remembered
Jim ramble on about grass,
how it heals over old gullies,
how it deepens the color
of the soil, the shine of
the coat, the eye, and how
that eye keeps its shape
there on the butcher's block.
"You can see yourself upside
down in the lens," Jim said.
"Your own face stares back."

And the road winds back
to the Divide where
the prairie takes a breath
rising up into the sky.
Here are the fields where

Jim followed the harvest,
corn bending to oats
to wheat in the Dakotas.
Chaff and grain, steam
rushing out with the pop
and hiss of the thresher,
smokestack black,
the farm woman driving
the wagon, reins in hands,
doubling in pain, easing
herself down to the ground
where Jim reached in,
caught her son, wrapped him
in his shirt, dark with sweat.
Chaff and grain,
the day's stubble still
on his skin, that night
Jim stretched out in the
bunkhouse, pockets turned
inside out by bad bets,
and felt the sky darken
and close, press down,
heard the rain hammer the roof.
He wrote a letter home:
he claimed he knew all
there was about animals.

He drifted on west and found
an abandoned farmhouse in

Montana with everything
he wanted—curtains, rugs,
books, dishes in the cupboard.
He settled in, sowed a few
potatoes, split firewood
for the winter with the ax
left in the stump.
But whenever he rode into town,
children pointed and whispered,
"That's the one
who lives in the house."
At the barber's, he finally
heard the story.

Jim:

An old geezer lived all his life in that place.
Never spent a cent and had sacks of the stuff
stashed somewhere, maybe buried in the yard.
Well, one day a tramp wandered around looking
for work and the old man set him to chopping wood.
Soon, the tramp whistled the geezer over,
wanting him to see the bugs drilling holes in the logs.
"Soon, they'll chew through your whole house," the tramp said.
"What, where?" the geezer wrinkled up his face.
The tramp pointed. "There. Get down on your knees
and you'll see." The geezer got down on all fours,
wheeled his neck around, trying to see them bugs.
Then the tramp swung, bringing the ax down,

7

whacking off the old man's head. Next, the tramp
rummaged through everything—even dug holes
in the yard and didn't turn up a dime,
so he skedaddled out of town, never to be seen again.
But the geezer. They said the geezer stalked the house
at night and nobody dared step a foot in the place
until I stumbled along. But I didn't see nothing.
Not at first. Until one day when I was splitting wood,
up walks the geezer, holding his head in his hands.
Said he'd give me all his dough if I'd go after that tramp—
had one side of his nose all smashed in.
He took me inside and lifted up the hearthstone
and pulled out a little bag of coins. I galloped out
the next day never intending to do no looking for nobody,
but in Green River, Wyoming, I fell into a poker game
with this tall scrawny fellow who was snorting funny
from a twisted-up nose. He skunked me clean—
every last coin in the bag, then waltzed toward
the door with the loot. "Stop right there!" I yelled
and pulled my gun (not knowing what I was going
to do then), when in walks the geezer carrying his head.
The tramp takes one look at the blood dripping
on the floor, starts to shake and shimmy and drops
over backwards. Stone dead. Me, I gathered up the coins
and trotted on home to begin my butcher shop in this town.

And in the morning
he lay his head down and told
you how the body fattens,

8

opens, the blood drains,
the hide peels from the skull,
the pink tongue turning purple,
split in two like a piece
of pine, the one clean hole
in the forehead drawing
the darkness in. He told
how the fat is scraped off,
rolled into a ball and
hung from a tree in late
fall for the birds,
how the fields close,
the pheasants gleaning
the few last seeds,
how the earth turns under,
then an explosion of wings
flies up in front of your face.

GEORGE

Uncle George smoked short
cigars and the night he died,
flicking ash on the floor,
said, "Reach under the cot,
honey, pull me out a beer."
Because he weighed only three pounds
at birth, Grandma kept him
in the oven for warmth,
and you still use the cake pan
she lay him in. At ten
he was kicked in the face
while castrating a horse
and George had one
glass eye from then on.
Winters, before a blizzard,
the socket throbbed and stung,
the lid rolling down like
a shade holding out the wind.
Summers, before a thunderstorm,
the eye swelled and blinked
up at you from the kitchen counter—
George afraid it would
explode in his head.

George smoked short cigars
and ground them out in
chicken-pecked barnyards while
the auctioneer waved his cane

through the air over:
milk cans and lard tins,
bridles and buckets,
buttons, thread,
First National Bank calendars,
hooks, rugs, ropes, pulleys,
hardback books on piglets and scours.

> *Five, five, who'll give*
> *me five, give me five?*

George bid a dollar
on a windowpane and

> *One, one, I got one, one,*
> *one, who'll make it two?*

another on an incubator,
and two on a weather vane,
but he didn't need the brass rooster
spinning round to know that
in the distance clouds were
charging across the fields.

> ("We'd just left the sale,"
> Edith Hill said in the *World Herald*,
> "when we lifted into the air—
> our old Chevy carried nearly

five miles—and would you believe it?
When we set down, we set down
right in front of our own house.")

And he didn't need the rooster
to tell him that Lyle Donavan
would keep up his song—
while the sky flashed yellow,
flashed purple—until every
last item was gone. So,
George waited, hands in pockets,
his one good eye on the horizon
while the other bidders
hugged the ground in the ditches
or ran for the cellar,
door slamming shut.
Later, through the rain,
you helped George pull home
a whole hayrack full
of loot for ten.

George smoked short cigars
and Grandma always cursed
and blamed them for sparking
the fire that burned down
all the buildings on the home place.
George squeezed his treasures
into a barn long since abandoned

by the cows, and their stalls
filled with washtubs,
hospital beds, a stuffed
two-headed calf.
Then every Sunday after dinner,
he disappeared to tinker:
nuts and bolts, a piece of wire,
copper kettle with coil.
"A little alcohol makes
a tractor run smoother."
George grinned at the heifer.
Soon, cars from all over
the county pulled into your lane,
headlights dim. Mason jars
glowed with the dark amber brew.
And because you were eight and
hands small, George had you
slip the extras into oil drums,
butter churns, and vacuum cleaner bags.
Once, when the sheriff came,
you even helped George into
the belly of an upright piano,
smoke rising from the lid.
"Put that out," you said,
and the strings twanged.
But you never saw smoke
rise so high, flames jumping
from barn to shed to house,

you never heard so many
buckets clank the night
the still blew.
Grandma leaned into the pump
and you ran water to the men
again and again, then
heard the rafters of the house
crack, tumble down through
the dining room,
felt the wind drive through
the grove, pushing the fire
into its own flame,
watched the moon rise over
the farm—George ambling down
the lane, to return only
one last time—and then all—
house, barn, shed,
piano, calf, coil—
collapsed into a circle of white ash.

JULIA

Julia was the first
at ten—and the priest
rode all the way from
Omaha to bless the ground—
part of a pasture Grandpa
fenced in. When you were
born, her stone sank
deep into the grass,
but Grandma would still
sit up at night with
her pipe and tell the story.

Grandma:

Her body trembled so,
slow at first, then Lord,
I thought it'd never stop.
Mouth fell open, eyes
and tongue rolled back.
Poor wee thing.
You just never knew when.
Could be in the field,
the barn, kneeling down
for prayers . . . Just like
the horses Jim brought home.
Each week he hitched up
a new one to my wagon.
Most trotted along fine,
then I'd be headed off to town

and all I'd remember were
my hands gripping the reins,
knuckles white, the stallions
bolting through the weeds . . .
We had to pick her up
from the floor, slip a
strap around each thigh,
pull it tight—that sent
the blood to her head—
and soon she lay limp
in my arms. In Ireland
they said the tinkers
stole those babies and
set them up in front
of the church with a cup.
So, I always kept her close,
tucked under my arm,
braced against a hip—
even though there was
none of that here—
or so I thought. Once,
when she was just beginning
to teeter around
the sod shanty,
I heard scuffling and
shuffling outside.
The door flew open and
four tall Sioux walked in.
A man scooped her up,

pulled off her clothes
and handed her around—
first to the men,
then the women,
two of each—until
the last wrapped her
in a buffalo blanket and
plunked her in my arms.
They left without saying
a thing, dropping a bag
of herbs on the bed: cinquefoil,
snakeroot and basswood leaves,
all to stop her shaking.
And they did.
She grew tall and thin,
then her heart began
to swell, to swell up
bigger than one of those
basswood leaves. You could
almost feel it open up
larger each spring,
push against her chest.
We were supposed to keep
her calm, but she was
always slipping off
to the barn trying to break
the ponies, tying their
tails together until
they kicked and bucked

until they finally gave up.
We tried to keep her calm,
hold her down, but it
was like the way
those Sioux made rope.
They stripped bark from
trees and soaked it
in a kettle with ash.
Time and again it'd float
to the top until they
weighed it with a stone,
and even then they'd find it
bobbing back. They used bark
for bandages, too,
but a forest couldn't cover
the wound I felt the day
the ground opened and
the ropes lowered her coffin.
My first daughter gone.
And the old life, too.
They said those tinkers
dug up their dead and
carried them with them.
But I knew then we'd build
a frame house here, plant
a grove for a windbreak.
On these plains there were
so few precious trees.

PHIL

We pull off Highway 30,
step in the Pine Grove Café,
pie case empty, chrome polished,
shiny as the capped teeth
of the woman behind the counter.
Her hands flutter to her face,
light falling through the window,
through the neon sign EAT,
light surrounding the loose
curls of her thin brown hair.

Overhead, the fan stirs
and our stools creak
as we study the menu
above the malt machine.
The prices are cheap.
"Eat up," you say, you'll treat,
and the woman stands ready
with pencil and pad.

I order the special and
her hands twitter from
nose to mouth to nose.

    "None today," she says.

You order a hamburger then.

    She looks at you and smiles.

"Sorry."

"Tenderloin?" I ask.

She shakes her head.

"Grilled cheese?"

"Sorry, sorry, we don't
sell food here anymore."

She explains that ever since
her husband died ten years back
she's opened every morning
for coffee but never again
fixed a single bite. Yet,
boots scrape under tables
and seed caps nod over heavy
steaming mugs and in the corner
two men talk about the corn,
how it stood up through all
this summer's horrible heat—
105° for five days straight—
and now we have a bumper crop
with grain piled in mounds
on the ground because the
trains don't run anymore

and a dime won't buy anything
much but a cup of coffee here.

You drink yours black and
talk about trains, how they
whizzed through town when
corn was a dime a bushel
and the weather so hot
and dry the hogs sat
in the sun all day like
old wooden tubs and
their skin cracked.
You talk about trains,
how Uncle Phil hoisted
one foot up, then hung
from the rod beneath
a boxcar and whistled down
the line through Amarillo,
Clovis, Roswell, Tucson,
Yuma, Los Angeles,
to drag a spoon across
a tin plate in the Sunshine
Mission and offer his flesh
to a pack of fleas in a flophouse.
Once, in Fresno he was thrown
in jail for stealing wine
from a nun, the swelling

on his head from the cop's stick
throbbing for ten days
as he lay on the floor
listening to his own ramblings
until Aunt Nell stood over him
with bail and Uncle George
with a bottle of rye.
Then the two men drank
their way to Reno and Colorado,
where they drifted into jobs
as hired hands and, *Crimers,*
you can still hear Phil say,
Colorado was the state where
I learned to housebreak hogs.

Phil:

We were there in the hog house
so's we could keep the sows from
rolling on their litters and, crimers,
after a while the smell got to you.
So, George told me I could train them hogs
same way I trained my dogs. Said I needed
to get up every morning at three
and walk them—one by one—down to
the old willow and back. So, I yanked
myself out, stumbling through the pasture,
shooing them hogs along in the dark,

calling *soo-ee, soo-ee,* until they did their duty.
But after a few weeks of this my eyelids
were slits by noon. So I put them critters
on their own. I tied a piece of steak
to the willow, then set a big banging
old alarm right down next to a sow's ear.
That night at three wham-bam the clock rang,
the sow woke and threw back her snout
charging toward the willow with the others
hightailing after. My plan worked 'cept
for one thing. I forgot to open the door,
and them critters busted right through,
pulling the whole house down, board by
board, until it was nothing but kindling.
Them hogs broke the house instead of
me housebreaking them.

After that Phil drove a
milk truck in Des Moines and
ran rum for Al Capone.
Had shotguns fit beneath his
running boards and sometimes
on trips across the state,
he'd stop for Sunday dinner.
Napkin tucked under chin,
he pushed his hand into his
pocket, tinkling with change.
He pressed a coin into your palm,

Buy yourself an ice cream cone.
Or sometimes, he spent the night
on the cot in the front room,
the mourning doves' song melting
into the hum of the fan,
windows open, trying to catch
any stir of leaves until the
old Milwaukee rumbled through
and Phil roared, "Crimers,
pick up your feet." The whole
house shook and then his litany
began, each huffing breath,
a piece of track:

>"Hail Mary, full of grace,
>the Lord is with thee.
>Blessed art thou amongst
>women and blessed is . . .
>*Ah, shit.*
>
>Holy Mary, mother of God,
>pray for us sinners now
>and at the hour of our death.
>*Ah, shit.*"

You were never certain
what happened at the hour
of Phil's death and Grandma

said never ask. One hot July day
the agent sent a message home:
Come to depot soon as possible.
You and Grandma hurried down,
a huge wooden crate
waiting on the platform.
With a crowbar,
Grandma pried open the lid
and pushed you into
the folds of her skirt.
But you saw enough.
You saw her reach in with
two shiny pennies for the eyelids.
You saw her place her
handkerchief over the face.
You saw the flies,
the bullet holes,
the bold lettering on the box:
PURE LARD.

The fan stirs and the woman
behind the counter swipes
a cloth across the burners
as if they were splattered
with grease. Her eyes flitter
open, shut, like the neon sign
hanging outside over our station wagon,
the body in back wrapped in

a grey blanket, strapped to a cot.
You stand to leave, pay the check,
a toothpick in your mouth.
I slip a few coins under
the saucer of my cup.

NELL

Grandma sent Aunt Nell,
the youngest girl, who
hated to cook, to cook
for each bachelor farmer
brother, their threshing crews,
spreading tables with chicken,
coleslaw, corn, serving up
bowls lumped full of mashed potatoes.

> "Want more, George?"
> "Believe I'll pass."
> *Plop.*
> "More, John?"
> "No, thank you, Nell. I don't
> care for potatoes."
> *Plop.*

Nell didn't care for
picky eaters, fancy clothes,
chatter. Her lips pressed
together straight as the edge of her
corn knife she held high then
let fall with one powerful whack,
chopping off the head of
a stewing hen. The bird flapped
about the yard and you watched
the blood spurt. You watched
Nell's hand slip in, return with
a lung, heart, gizzard,

the stones inside ground smooth
as the gravel under the tracks
of the old Milwaukee,
the train that carried her to
Colorado in 1910 with her brother,
Uncle Charlie, his head on
her shoulder, his lungs filling
with blood. The air was better
in the mountains and she hoped
for a cure. So, for nearly
a year they lived in a tent
pitched at the foot of Pike's Peak.
Mornings, they wandered the
woods with a field guide and
learned the names of the wildflowers:
meadow rue, prairie smoke or
old man's whiskers.
She was eighteen,
he twenty-two.
They searched for morels
on the south side of dead trees—
hollowed-out elm, fallen pine—
and when they found a batch,
they kept their secret
curled inside themselves.
Afternoons, he slept and
she carried water

from the lake, gathered twigs
and branches for a fire.
Birch, aspen, oak.
She studied the twigs,
their leaf-scars, and learned
that trees could be known from
their branches even without
leaves or flowers or fruit.
Evenings, they ate, then
wrapped themselves in blankets
and rubbed their hands over
the coals. They sang:

> *Oh, where you go, I want to go,*
> *and a fair wind blow.*
> *Oh, hey, oh, ho,*
> *oh, hey, oh, ho,*
> *and a fair wind blow.*

Then Charlie's long thin arms
grew longer and thinner
as they wound around Nell's waist
at night when he couldn't sleep
for the cough and she felt
a canyon open, a few loose
pieces of stone slip in.
Then you remember them home

again and we have the photo
in the album of the two
in the buggy, the reins in
her hands, his shoulders
curved, chest caved in,
dark eyes staring out
beneath the rim of his
derby hat. Then you remember
Nell folding up the cot
in the front room, and
day by day, her back
rounding to a stoop,
limbs growing lighter
until her body was a shape
taking on the shape
of the field, stubble under
her feet, cornstalks down,
voice low :

> *Oh, hey, oh, ho—*
> *and a fair wind blow* ...

When the snow fell,
Grandma sent her to Oregon
to live with friends and
sell books. Nell spent a year
rising every day at dawn,

knocking door to door,
then shuffling across dance floors
at night, dining on fresh salmon
and crab until the hollows
in her cheeks filled and her
letters home lengthened with
details of the ocean, mountains,
the incense cedar with its
tiny scale-like leaves pressed
close to stems, winding up into
the open air, letting go of
its blossoms in January.
In February Grandma brought
her home to help nurse Uncle John.

At eighty, after burying
all brothers, sisters, parents,
and husband, Doc,
Nell still raised chickens
and incubated a brood each spring
in the furnace room.
I helped teach them to drink,
dipping one beak, then another,
in a jar lid of water.
Then they were yellow,
then brown, fluff slicking
to feathers as we turned

the heat lamp dimmer,
then off, setting them out
in the sun every warm afternoon.

We hardened the cabbage plants
that way, too, lifting the
leaf mulch, easing them into
the garden dirt, and when
the corn dried and curled,
potatoes in baskets,
we boiled up the jars,
screwed down the lids,
lined the walls of the
fruit cellar with blue glass.
In the dark winter, wind up,
windows sealed, roads closed,
each jar shone in our hands,
the peaches drifting together,
apart, like continents.

At eighty, Nell rocked in
Grandma's old horsehair stuffed
chair and we sat with her in
the front room, the fat beagle
at her feet, rosary in hand.
A log burned in the fireplace,
radio on mantel, volume turned up
so loud Father Maloy's voice

boomed down April Street
toward May. She mumbled back
each response, consonants
slurred (teeth fitting better
now in the cup), then blessed
herself again while the
program switched to polka.

Nell:

Don't you see, folks come over here now,
set right there and say,
Nell, why don't you travel?
Got nothing to hold you.
Can't leave the furnace, I say.
Fire might go out, pipes freeze.
But wouldn't it be nice to get out
of the cold just one time?
I say someone's got to shovel coal.
Well, why don't you
convert to gas?
Only person in town still
digging out clinkers.
But I need them ashes
for my garden and chickens.
The spring then.
My lettuce'd bolt.
The rabbits'd chomp

through my beans.
Or summer.
But I wouldn't want to miss
putting up my tomatoes and corn.
Besides, I drove to Coon Rapids
this spring to buy fence,
and to Cherokee this summer
for May Burke's funeral.
But don't you see, they want me
to take a train, see the desert
in bloom, see Europe, Africa, the Far East.
I say I've seen scenery.

MAUD

You and Nell found Aunt Maud
stretched on a cot
in her farmhouse,
five or six dogs piled on top,
and to carry the body out
you plunked down boards
so your feet wouldn't sink
through the ankle-deep poop.
I remember Maud's place—
the narrow path that led
through the three-room shack,
the piles of books and Des Moines *Registers*,
the Wonder Bread wrappers
folded and stacked to the ceiling,
braided into rugs on the floor.
Slices were toasted on top
the cookstove, then spread
with peanut butter.
Slices were dipped in milk and egg,
fried, and drowned in maple syrup.
Slices were crumbled and scattered
in the snow for the juncos,
were broken into a bowl
for the dogs, tossed whole
to the hogs in the barn.
When Nell and I visited,
we bounced down the lane, rolling
up the windows, the dogs
charging the car, tails down,

teeth set in a sneer.
Nell honked and Maud shuffled
out on the porch, shouting,
"Here, Prince."
(Maud had a string of seven
different dogs named Prince.)
"Don't know what's gotten
into that dog."
I swung open the car door
and the pack sniffed and licked
my pant leg until I scurried into
the house, where Nell and I
teetered from one leg to the other
in the tiny kitchen—
there wasn't a chair to sit—
and Maud pulled out a piece
of her moldy bread and
offered us grilled cheese.
"Believe I'll pass," Nell said.

I remember Maud's place
but you say that was only the last.
As she grew older and richer,
flesh puffing from frame,
she moved again and again,
each house smaller and shabbier,
further from town,

each house taking in one more dog.
"Here, Prince," she called,
hoisting herself into her jeep,
the pack squeezed in around her,
drooling on the seats,
the dash, her canvas cape
that flapped in the wind
as she raced down the gravel road
and roared into your drive
to collect the rent.
(Grandpa had left her twenty acres
and soon twenty grew to eighty
to half the county
and she charged you
to live on the home place.)
Prince snapped at your hand
as Maud huffed and groaned
and pried herself out from
behind the wheel, her cape hiking up
just enough for you to see
that underneath she was naked.

Home, she hosed down the cape
and hung it over the porch railing
where every Sunday morning
she picked up her copy of
The New York Times,

and in the afternoon lay
on her cot and sang along
with the radio,
squeaking out the arias
and recitatives
with the singers from the Met.
Once, at nineteen she married
and ran off to Chicago
with a fertilizer salesman,
but came back in six months,
claiming the city unsafe.
(But Grandma said that's where
she picked up all her Eastern airs.)
Once, Prince trembled when Maud
whistled him into her jeep
for their daily trip to town.
He hid under the porch steps
and the rest of the pack
closed round, so Maud choked
the engine and left them behind,
zooming toward town, running
her usual stop sign,
rounding Kussell's corner,
never looking left nor right at the tracks.
Suddenly, she was in the air,
rising, floating,

her body light as if full of holes.
Then she was punched down
again into her jeep,
the train still blasting its horn,
and she felt her wind rush out,
lungs fold in, her leg snap.
After that, she dragged one foot
as she hobbled around the shack,
and what was left of the jeep
sank into the mud down by the creek.
She quit going
to church but made the priest
ride out every First Friday
with the sacrament. Things were
in English by then,
and when Father Maloy held
the host in front of her face—
"This is my Body"—
she refused to say, "Amen."
You drove there
with the rent check and sometimes
found the two dark eyes
of a shotgun aimed out the window,
or sometimes you found Maud
on the tractor in the field,
circling round and round,

neither plowing nor planting,
the sun beating down on her naked back.
Once, you found her sitting
cross-legged on the cot, eyes fixed.
She didn't hear you come in.
She didn't even blink
when you put your hand on her arm.
She just began to talk.

Maud:

There was a ewe killed down at old man
Sullivan's place. He came knocking saying
a pack of neighbor dogs done it and
would I help him round them up.
I fetched my gun then we headed off
to Burke's and took care of Old Shep.
Then to Kunkle's and Kussell's and Fink's,
but when we got to Mammy Flannery's,
she swore up and down that her little
rat terrier ain't done nothing.
"Oh," she wailed, "not him, not him."
She begged and begged me but Sullivan
already had him cornered in the barn
and Mammy fell to a pool at my feet
when she heard the shot. Then I headed home.
And found Prince.
Oh, he done it all right. Still had

the blood dribbling down his chin.
But up until then he was the best I'd ever had.
I trained that Prince.
I taught him to come and sit and heel,
and then he used to be my dishwasher.
I'd put my plate down on the floor and
lickety-split, it'd be clean.
In the morning I'd poke my head out
the window and holler, "Prince,"
and he'd come wagging and I'd want
a certain sow and all I had to do was point
and Prince'd nose her out. But I took him
down by the creek and set him up on the bank.
Jesus. He perched up there just a-grinning,
his ears pointing as I raised my gun.
Well, there's one thing.
I should've dug the hole first.
I should've dug the hole first.

When they dug Maud's hole,
they went way down toward the end,
clear of everyone, and the priest
said that's where she belonged,
willing all her money to her dogs.
And when they lowered her in,
no one knew how long she'd been gone.
She didn't believe in a phone
and would go for weeks without

seeing a person.
At the wake they kept
the coffin lid shut and
you never told anyone what you
found that day you stepped
on the porch, the dogs whining,
bowls empty, ribs sticking out.
You knew by the stench,
but never told how you covered
your face with a handkerchief
when you and Nell bent over the body,
and how the body had turned black,
as if a stain had spread over the skin,
and how the hands were folded across
the chest and little bits of flesh
on the fingertips were nibbled away
like crumbs of bread.

DOC

Doc sent his hopeless here
to the Grotto of the Redemption.
We pull into the lot and
park near the Stations of the Cross,
each scene pieced together with
moonstone, opal, jade.
You say we'll stop
for Father Grieving's blessing,
and soon we are kneeling
under the Beatitudes,
his hands on my shoulders,
the way they rested on
Doc's arthritic, asthmatic, insane.

> "Yak-a-wa-kaw-do-oh-ma-da,
> la-la-loop-pa-wa-key-no-way-na-ma."

His eyes roll toward the sky
as he speaks in tongues.

> "Ha-wa-wa-dee-da-way-he-no-way,
> fo-moo-lue-see-we-day-no-fay."

He guides us to the Shrine of the Virgin,
her marble face serene,
eyes, rubies, staring down
at the water dripping
from her hands

pressed together in prayer,
water falling through the air,
each drop adding one more
deposit to the stalagmite
rising from the floor.
He tells us how
it all began here
with a woman in a wheelchair,
her lips moving silently
to the rosary,
her fingers too cramped
and twisted to hold the beads.
"May I pray with you?" he said,
and then their voices rose in unison.

> "Glory be to the Father,
> and to the Son, and to the Holy Ghost . . ."

and as they travelled the decades,
the mysteries,

> "As it is now and ever shall be,
> world without end. Amen."

he felt a light spread
through his bones,
his muscles, move out his skin,

filling the shrine.
Then the woman rose, slowly.
One step. Two. Three.
She shuffled forward.
"Glory be," she murmured.
"Glory be," she shouted. "Glory be!"

After a few years the shrine
filled with old wheelchairs,
hearing aids,
braces, crutches,
and you remember Edith Hill
interrupting Sunday dinner again
and Doc suggesting that maybe
Father Grieving could do more
for her lockjaw than he.
Well, when Edith came home
chomping and chattering,
she darted down Main Street
to the Corner Café
and soon even the Methodists
began to make the trip:
Shorty Long with his lumbago,
Gloomy Heinz with his swollen prostate,
Putt-Putt McNut with his harelip.
But in the middle of the night
Doc still cranked up his old Ford,

blasted his blowtorch
under the engine to warm it,
and drove out the country roads
through the snowdrifts,
stopping to shovel, stopping
to hook up his chains,
gloves sticking to metal,
driving on, fighting the wind,
searching for the place
with the lantern on the gate.
And inside the house,
the woodstove huffed
in the kitchen
but the stuff in the cupboards
was frozen, and in the back room,
a woman huddled under the quilt,
temperature 104°.
Lobar pneumonia.
She pulled through with
what Doc left: tincture digitalis,
Brown's cough syrup, codeine.
And Doc pulled down the roads again
on into spring
with the storms and mud
and Mammy Flannery ramming
logs into her cookstove,
steam rising from kettles,
and Tillie with her first
upstairs in the dark bedroom,

rain leaking through the ceiling,
Doc rolling up his sleeves
and Mammy holding an umbrella
over his head. After twelve hours,
"Now push, now, push, push, push,"
the baby finally came and was fine,
but no matter how hard they worked,
the afterbirth just wouldn't budge.
Then Mammy was on the stairs,
tramping in with a beer bottle.
"Here, girl, blow," she said.
Tillie threw back her head
and blew hard,
then the placenta shot out intact
and Mammy carried it to the garden
to mulch the roses.
Doc slipped the bottle into his bag
and took it with him
then to every birth.

When his daughter, Rita,
turned sixteen, Doc handed over
the wheel and blowtorch
to her and together
they drove down the gravel road
and around the washout, creek swollen,
water backed up in the ditches.
When they slowed at the stop sign,
she stretched out her left arm

for a turn,
and Doc put out his right,
then stomped his foot
into the floorboard.
"Give it the gun," he said
as they charged up
the muck-rutted hill
to the gypsy camp
where a man lay in a tent,
left ear sheared off,
hanging by the lobe.
In the dim lantern light,
Rita threaded the needle
and Doc sutured
cartilage and scalp,
and when they finished,
a woman dropped two gold pieces
in his bag.
When they drove out again
for the stitches,
the tent was gone,
but back in the office
they found another gold piece
tied up in a scarf
with tiny bits of thread.
"Ear must've stuck on," was all Doc said.
And that afternoon he cut Billy Kunkle's leg off.
Old man Kunkle ran a sawmill

south of town and one morning
he and the boy rushed into
the office, Billy's right shoe
covered with blood.
Doc pulled off Billy's muddy pants
and when he peeled away his hightops,
his right foot was left
in his shoe, the bare stump
of his leg sticking out.
Doc wanted to amputate
below the knee to make
a good fit for an artificial foot,
but old man Kunkle said,
"No, leave him with what he's got."
So, Doc cleaned and dressed
the wound and sent him off
with a tetanus shot.
A few days later,
Doc walked over to check
and as soon as he entered
the front room,
he smelled the gangrene.
This time the old man agreed,
and to stop the growth,
Doc sawed above the knee,
but sewed up Billy
a good stump and
was always proud after that

when he watched the boy
amble down the street with barely a limp.

When Doc had his stroke,
he was knocked right off his feet.
Months before, beer bottles
had spilled out of his bag,
out of George's barn,
off shelves and into glasses.
It was the Depression and
he was getting paid with chickens.
Then Uncle Sam shipped him
down to Arkansas to care for
a CCC full of hungry men
and there's the picture of him
in the album—jodhpurs and boots,
Mountie-type hat—his face swollen,
cheeks sagging like the roof
of the cabin behind him.
And that's where it happened—
the dizziness, the headache,
the cabin steps, the trees
blurring, multiplying by two,
his own right limbs
weighing down, going numb.
Nell sent you and Rita
to drive him home
and Doc lay on a stretcher

in the back of the Ford
while the two of you sped
the thirty-hour trip non-stop.
Rita kept checking Doc's breathing
and once when she thought
it had stopped, his chest heaved.
"Give it the gun," he sighed.
At home, Nell stationed him
on the cot before the bay window,
the breeze coming through the screen.
On a hot August afternoon
Doc watched the neighbor children
playing in the yard,
the grass damp with mist.
It felt like rain and Doc thought
the children like cattle
under the tree, raising,
lowering their white faces
as if from some meadow pool.
He thought of his childhood
farm in Ireland,
how it stretched out over the sea,
how now in the heat the children's
bodies looked like the rocks below.
He thought of the sounds inside
his chest, the snap and pull
of the water hitting the rocks.
Then first he saw the boy,

the bat, Billy Kunkle racing
toward first base, weight shifting
from foot to stump,
the other children moving back,
their gloves in front of their faces,
blotting the sun,
waiting for the smooth arc of the fungo,
the ball spinning,
stitches fraying, sutures
loosening the leather flap.
Then Billy's bad leg
was in the hole,
twisting, snapping,
a tiny blood clot in his stump swimming
into his vein, speeding
toward his heart.
Then the boy was on the ground,
the children running toward
the house, Doc rising on one elbow,
shouting through the screen,
"My God. I can't get up!"
Then Nell was in the yard,
picking up the boy.
The other children began
to disappear, one by one,
their faces a blur.
Doc could hear only the noise

of the locusts drumming
against the screen.
He could see the boy
running again, falling to the ground.
He could see the boy
racing toward first base,
his foot in the hole,
sinking further and further
into the earth.
He could feel the lawn
open around him, fill like a pool.

"Yak-a-wa-ma-kaw-do-oh-ma-da,
la-la-loop-pa-wa-key-no-way."

Father Grieving sprinkles holy water
on us, circles the car,
blessing the body in the back.

"Thou shalt sprinkle me with hyssop,
O Lord, and I shall be cleansed:
Thou shalt wash me, and I shall
be made whiter than snow.

May almighty God have mercy on you,
forgive you your sins, and bring you
to life everlasting. Amen.

May the almighty and merciful Lord
grant your servant, Rita, pardon,
absolution, and forgiveness of
all her sins. Amen."

Father hugs each of us good-bye,
then I turn over the engine
and back out past the Ten Commandments,
past the Archangels Michael and Gabriel,
flicking on the wipers
to whisk away the drops
of holy water that dot
the windshield like rain.

ED

"I'm not retired,
just damn tired," Uncle Ed said
as he sat in his feed and seed store
down on Main Street, coughing up
"little Rocky Mountain oysters" of phlegm.
(Ed'd lost his own to cancer.)
But in the end, it was his heart
that gave out, ankles swelling up
bigger than a "heifer's heinie."
And that's when he bought his cane—
a bull's dong, stiffened, stretched,
and lacquered, with a little
black rubber tip on the end.
Back and forth, he tapped
from the store, where the boys
still gathered at ten in the morning
for their pinochle game,
to the Corner Café at noon,
where Thelma served up a bowl
of her homemade chicken soup.
And Ed knew all about chickens.
He kept several hundred
on his place just outside town.
They ran loose in the yard,
out into the road, on back
into the house. Grandma used
to send Nell to clean, but finally
she refused, and after fifteen years,

Ed bought a trailer, set it up
inside the gate, and gave the house to the birds.
Once, a couple of cousins from
New Jersey passed through and
Ed moved in another trailer,
tacking a sign on the door, VISITORS.
When they used the outhouse,
he warned them to leave the door
open long enough to let the skunk out,
but close it fast enough
to keep the bobcat from getting in.
(And that was the last we heard
from that part of the family.)
After the war, at fifty,
Ed married Fanny.
            ("Real name's Louise," Ed said.
             "But when I met her, she was in
              the field working her fanny off,
              so I called her Fanny.")

Right away they had a baby
and bought yet another trailer for her.
And just the way a mother
knows her baby's cry,
Ed knew his chickens' shit.

Ed:

Sheriff found a steer sliced to hell
down by Catfish Creek. Come round
and con-fer-scated everything
in the county that could cut.
Up and down the road he went
and took my chain saw.
Now I ask you, if I was a-going
to carve the tongue out of a critter
in the middle of the night,
would I use a chain saw?
Have to be dumber than Old Shep.
But he signed mine in just the same,
and when it came time for everyone
to go down and claim their tools—
(Never did find the culprit, neither.
Some said witchcraft.
Others, Martians in a UFO,
but I don't know.
Naw ... I'd say some of them old hippies.
I knew how to set them down and talk turkey.
"Why don't you cut your hair?" I'd ask.
"Jesus had long hair," they said.
"Yup. But that was before they invented scissors.")
When the time came for me to fetch my saw,
sheriff said did I have the serial number?
Hell, no, I ain't got no number.
Then how am I to know your saw

from Shorty Long's or Putt-Putt McNut's?
Simple, I said. See that one there?
That's my chicken shit on it.
Rhode Island Reds.
I know'd my saw. I know'd my shit anywhere.

Ed knew his chickens and he knew
his ducks. Every morning
he stepped out of his trailer
with a bucket of corn, stuck his fingers
in his mouth and whistled.
Then they lifted into the air,
some from the creek, some from the fields.
Round and round above the house,
the mallards circled, their glossy-green heads,
white neck-rings, shining.
Then they lit down next to his feet,
slipping kernels from his hand.
In the fall, during hunting season,
Ed shut them up in the visitors' trailer,
and they stayed all winter,
bleating out their calls over the snow.
Inside his trailer,
geraniums blooming in the windows,
Ed spent the long dark nights
studying birds. Bent over books,
he read out loud to Fanny
about the male red-bellied woodpecker
tapping inside his nest hole

to attract a mate, the female alighting
outside, tapping her answer.
He read about the dull-colored
bowerbirds building tent-like nests,
painting them with twigs poked into berries.
He put the record on the phono
and sometimes you stopped by to listen—
Roger Tory Peterson identifying bird calls:

Garooo-a-a-a

        Sandhill Crane

Garooo-a-a-a

Oong-ka'choonk, oong-ka'choonk, oong-ka'choonk

        American Bittern

Oong-ka'choonk, oong-ka'choonk, oong-ka'choonk

Once, Ed ran unopposed
to the State Legislature and
the Democrats used him to filibuster.
Ed stood for hours on the House floor:

Weeta weeta wit-chew

        Magnolia Warbler

Weeta weeta wit-chew

Ti-dee'-di-di

American Goldfinch

Ti-dee'-di-di

Summers, Ed paid every kid
in town a nickel for each butterfly named.
Monarchs, admirals, swallowtails,
sulphurs and skippers, we dashed
around the cemetery and railroad cut
with jars and nets.
Home, we spread wings on Styrofoam,
anchoring pins beneath veins,
careful not to rub the scales
and blur the eyespots.
I went on to bees, wasps, ticks,
but when I brought Ed a whole
coffee can full of rattlers,
he said the bank was broke.
In the fall, after school,
we gathered in Ed's store for other lessons.

"Know how to refinish furniture?" Ed asked.

Popping the cap off a bottle of Coke,
he brushed aside some papers,
then poured the liquid all over his desk.

. . .

"Let that soak in real good, now."

It dribbled over the edge
and onto the floor.
It ran into his papers,
flooding piles of receipts.
It oozed and fizzed
around the corners of the register.
Ed pulled an old bandana from his pocket.

"Then wipe it off, and see how that
cleans it up? See how it cleans it up?"

Ed's bandana was black with dust and dirt.

"Now you'll want some shine.
Know what makes the best polish?"

I shook my head.

"Do you know?"

I shrugged.

"It's Vaseline. Yup, Vaseline."

Ed took a jar of the stuff
from his desk drawer

and smeared it on the wood.
He rubbed it into the desk
with the flip side of his bandana.

"There. Run your hand there."

My fingers grazed the desk
and stuck to the oak.

"Ain't that the smoothest finish
you ever saw? Well, ain't it?"

Ed's next trick was real magic.
He put on his black cape and top hat,
twirling around two or three times.
Then we lined up across the store,
holding hands, stringing out
between the seed potato barrel
at one end of the place
and the atrazine at the other.
Then he put a funnel to my ear
and poured in a cup of milk.
And, tapping, *abber-cadaver, one, two, three,*
the milk traveled across the store,
down the line, from kid to kid,
until it spilled out Ronnie Mittendorf's pant leg,
and the cat lapped it from the floor.
"Felt like I was peeing in my pants," Ronnie grinned.

. . .

When Ed began to leak,
he drove himself to Vets hospital
where he'd been two or three times
a year since the war,
his old $300 Chevy (purchased from an ex-nun)
revved, rust holes in the fenders patched
with duct tape,
St. Christopher medal stuck to the dash,
wings shooting out from the Christ child's globe.
Ed lit a cigarette, snapped on
the country station,
and over the back roads,
gravel to blacktop,
sang along with his favorite song:

Oh, the rain's coming down
and the roof won't hold her.
I lost my job,
and I feel a little older.

Work your fingers to the bone,
what'ya get?
Bony fingers, bony fingers.

The urology ward was almost too small
to hold Ed after his operation
as he roamed the halls in a wheelchair,
shouting at the doctors and nurses
to clear the way,

stopping in on Gloomy Heinz
to stir up a card game,
imitate a yellow-bellied sapsucker,
or pull five or six silk scarves
from his pajama bottoms.
"Bony fingers," he sang.
"Bony fingers," he sang as he drove
himself home, then back again and again
as his body continued to break down,
but you can still hear his cane tapping
Main Street as he came home at last
from his last stay.

Ed:

Men of the Cavalry, deal.
Me? The ticker not the plumbing.
Hell, I'm already a gelding.
No, I come in for my yearly and just when
they wired me to the electro-heart-i-o-graph,
blam, it went off. Wanted to shut the gate
on me then, but I needed to go home
and feed Fanny—an invalid, you know—
rheumatoid. So, I drove out the lot
and it all went black, busted
right through the arm and bent my antenna back.
I'll take two. Never been so dizzy, neither,
'cept for the time in number one when
I ran horses across the border

from Mexico, me full of tequila
(sixteen, lied to sign up),
bottles stuffed down in the saddlebags.
See you one, raise you one.
In number two I never rode nowhere
'cept in a wheelchair. Soon as I volunteered,
meningitis spread through the barracks
like the blight, each man's spine
curling under. Put me in quarantine,
head hanging down from the table
till they stabbed me in the cord.
But I'll take the needle any day
over the buggy whip. In sixty
they rammed it down my throat
to take a look at my gut,
then zipped out half my stomach
and I don't know what.
Filmed it in living color, too,
then rolled it every year for them interns.
I never missed a show.
Five separate times I seen my belly sewed up.
See you two, raise you two.
Now they want to butcher me again,
but this time I told them to shove it.
Oh, they claim I'll be bad for only two weeks,
then so's I can pull right up in front
of Hy-Vee, they'll give me one of them blue tags
with the rocking chair hanging down,

but I said, naw . . .
I seen them guys in here yipping and yapping
in pain, double and triple bypass.
I seen the priest swaying over them,
waving his hands through the air.
See you three, raise you one.
No, sir. If I wanted Tef-a-lon,
I'd go out and buy me a fry pan.

GRANDMA

"Raspberries.
I'm hungry for raspberries,"
Grandma said as she lay on the cot
in the cellar.
In her later years,
she'd grown more and more
afraid of someone breaking in
(one of those tinkers, maybe)
and carting off the sterling and crystal,
the whole houseful of furniture.
"They'll cut through the screen
and crawl right in that window,"
she knew, so she drove long
nails into the storms and
kept them up winter and summer,
the place sweltering by August,
the only escape left underground.
One hand groping the railing,
the other toting berries,
you edged down the steps
and called her name.
"Here I am," a voice rose
through the dark, and you
spotted her propped on
the cot in the corner,
stomach swelling higher
each day from the cancer.
And the odor stronger, too,

a little like bread dough.
And now she could eat nothing,
yet hour after hour she
moaned for raspberries.
So, you took turns in the garden,
gathering fruit from canes.
Until the end,
you put a bowl beside the cot
even when Grandma's eyes glazed,
lips parched, and she could only
open her mouth enough to
whisper and call you Delia,
her dead sister's name.
And until the end,
the townspeople came—
old and young—
to buy her herbs and
try the cures she'd learned
from the Indians:
sage for sore throats,
bloodroot for colds,
dandelion for female organs.
Some even remembered Grandma
during the plagues—typhoid
and diphtheria—when she stayed
awake for days, trudging

from farm to farm with
her compresses and teas,
and dragging home in the morning
to strip by the gate,
boiling her dress before
entering her own house.
But most remember her
as midwife (before Doc
came to town), tramping down
the road from way off,
smoke pouring from her pipe.
They waited and watched
until she got close,
and if she were swinging
her little bag, they said,
"Here comes Grandma
carrying somebody a baby."

Grandma:

In that bag I had matches and scissors,
a bottle of holy water and
a good piece of linen. That's all.
I snipped the cord, lit a fire,
then cut up a piece of the cloth
and scorched it—put it on a shovel

and held it over the flames until
it was nice and brown like a turkey skin.
Then I poked a hole and pulled the navel
cord through, left the cloth next to the belly
like that until the cord rotted off.
Three, four, five days.
Always afraid I wouldn't fix it right,
but in all those years, I never missed
a time. And you could be sure,
if they was going to go,
it'd be from that cord.
That or the croup.
And, honey, I seen them born
blue as the earth. Choke t'death,
that's what, if you don't grab them
and shake them and blow down their throats.
Cut loose the phlegm. And if the mother
didn't have enough milk, I brewed
catnip tea and gave her a dose of
castor oil. Pay?
Maybe a twist of tobacco for my pipe,
or a pumpkin or two, and then they
always knew I was fond of raspberries.

So, one by one, the townspeople
came to the cellar, sat beside
her and held her hand
like she'd done with them.

"Nothing that's born," she'd said,
"is born without pain."
And then in the dark
her face was barely visible.

　　　　"Have you come for a cure or
　　to confess your sins?"
　　　　"A cure. But I have sinned in
　　my life, Grandma."
　　　　"Oh? What have you done?"
　　　　"Well, I've smoked a little.
　　Will that keep me out of heaven?"
　　　　"No. Smoking won't keep you out.
　　What else you done?"
　　　　"I've taken a drink or two. Will
　　drinking keep me out of heaven?"
　　　　"Drinking won't. What else you done?"
　　　　"I've taken a chew once or twice.
　　Will chewing keep me out?"
　　　　"No. You can go to heaven if you
　　chew, but you have to go to hell to spit."

You were sure Grandma went to heaven.
Her dying was so long and hard,
the priest came around
three different times,
running through all your cotton balls.
Once, when her breathing and pulse

slowed, the whole family
huddled in the cellar,
candles flickering,
just like the time the twister
ripped up the town.
Then her lungs filled and
you pulled phlegm from her throat.
The rattle began and the flush
spread across her face
while her hands and feet
turned blue.
You were only twelve and had
always been told first you'd hear
the wind, then the low blasting
noise like a train going through,
then the rain, and the rain
would mean the all-clear sign.
But when the family shuffled
back up the cellar steps,
there was no rain, nothing
was clear, nothing settled.
Her dying went on and Nell
slipped outside for another
bowl of raspberries. Grandma
fell into a deep sleep
only to waken at two that
morning, shaking,
stuttering, eyes wide.

Grandma:

I've seen Death.
With long grey hair almost to her waist,
a black dress pulled tight at her breast.
She was walking the back roads and stopped
near a window.
It was early morning,
the light bright.
She floated toward me through the glass
and laid something at my feet—tiny, sharp,
a scissors, I thought, but then it opened
into the shape of a crucifix. She glided away
back down the road, then paused and called,
"Pick up your cross and follow me."

After that Grandma shoved her cot
over close to the window,
kept her rosary dangling
from the rafter above her head,
her scapular pressed against her chest.
And her dying went on.
For days she lay awake and
as her fever rose, she called
over and over for her father,
for her mother.
Then her arms and legs straightened,
flesh stung, muscles stiffened

and jerked as if they were
bound by cord.

        "Let me go," she pleaded.
        "Cut me loose. Cut me loose."

        Once, to comfort her, Maud took her
        hand and said,
            "There, you're free."
            "Where? In heaven?"
            "Yes. You're in heaven."
            "No, I ain't. If you're there,
        too, then I ain't."

When Grandma finally went,
they made you stay upstairs.
It was 103° and the air so wet
your undershirt stuck,
but what you remember most
was the low thump-thud
like the wind banging
the screen door shut,
then the noise growing
louder and louder again
until every room in the house
gurgled and knocked.
"It was her heart," Nell said

at last from top the cellar steps.
"It just wouldn't quit."
They stretched Grandma out
on a board in the fruit room
so she'd keep and washed her,
under the arms, over the abdomen
(then the size of a pregnant woman's),
down between the legs,
and it was then you noticed
the birthmark on her buttock
the same size, shape
and place as yours.
They stuffed her rectum
and vagina with cotton,
massaged her face so her eyes
would shut and kept her lids
pressed down with nickels.
In the coal room, they found
the black dress she'd made,
and right away before
the rigor mortis set in,
they slit it down the back
and slipped it on, while
Uncle Jim began pulling
dry boards from the loft
in the barn and the sound
of saw teeth biting pine

rose through the air and
joined with the tolling
of St. Anthony's bell.

"Do you have the dress?"
you ask as the road winds
toward town and we head in to
the Odis Funeral Home.
I point at the paper sack,
then Frankie Odis wants to know
if it's all there—my mother's
stockings, pants, bra.
I nod and he leads us down
a stairway to the cellar,
where ten caskets nose in
close to each other.
One long, shiny black.
Another oak.
A pink one with pink rhinestones
and lace. We walk among them,
then I remember running down
the block again to Frankie's house,
ringing the bell,
and since there isn't
a body in the parlor,
we scamper downstairs,
Frankie hiding his eyes,
counting one, two, three, four . . .
I dash around the room

until in the back
behind a curtain, I find
a small plain brown one,
hop in and pull the lid down.
Now, Frankie, at twenty-five,
has been to embalming
school and he tells us
how the black comes with a
moisture-proof vault, how the oak
has an especially good gasket,
how the pink has class.
But I suggest the brown,
and when he rolls it out from
behind the curtain, you agree.
Next, we pick the holy card
and take the Sacred Heart with
its flames and crown of thorns,
and then I remember the picture
in the album, baptism,
the bleeding Jesus over the font.
You hold my head up, taking
my part for each response
as the priest pours the water
and drives the devil out.
And there's the shot next to that
of our boat at the lake,
water pouring in the bottom,
you with a coffee can bailing.
6 a.m., and my first fishing

expedition, you still in your
nightgown, an old trench coat
pulled over the top.
"Row toward the bank some,"
you say, thinking you spot
a green heron in the shade.
My foot on the bar, I pull
back on the oars and we glide near.
You focus your binoculars,
leaning closer, his long neck,
shaggy crest in sight.
You lean closer, then *skyow, skewk,*
you are under, head bobbing,
flapping your arms until
I catch hold of your coat belt
and reel you in.
And when Frankie asks about
the cemetery plot, I see my mother
going under, hear the clouds
break loose, the rain pelt down.
You stand with me again under
the canopy in your plastic
bonnet drawn tight under the chin.
We watch the incense circle
up into the sky, wait for
the priest, the acolytes,
all the other mourners to leave,

and say one last prayer together.
Then we tramp down the row,
you bending to pull some weeds
grown up around Jim's stone,
vowing to do a rubbing of Julia's,
her dates so dim. When we reach
the end where the land drops off
into the railroad cut, mud sliding down,
raspberries tangling up, our eyes
measure the space and you say
there's enough room at least
for you and me.

A NOTE ABOUT THE AUTHOR

Mary Swander was born in 1950 in Carroll, Iowa, and was educated at Georgetown University, the University of Iowa, and the University of Iowa Writers' Workshop. She has taught at Lake Forest College and the Interlochen Arts Academy, and currently conducts workshops for the University of Iowa in both poetry and therapeutic massage.

A NOTE ON THE TYPE

This book was set on the Linotype in Century Expanded,
designed in 1894 by Linn Boyd Benton (1844–1932).
Benton cut Century Expanded in response to Theodore
De Vinne's request for an attractive, easy-to-read typeface to fit the narrow columns of his *Century Magazine*.
Early in the nineteen hundreds Morris Fuller Benton
updated and improved Century in several versions for
his father's American Type Founders Company. Century is the only American typeface cut before 1910
that is still widely in use today.

Composed, printed, and bound by Heritage
Printers, Charlotte, North Carolina
Designed by Virginia Tan